The Library of Healthy Living™

Staying Healthy:

Good Hygiene

Alice B. McGinty

The Rosen Publishing Group's
PowerKids Press™
New York

Published in 1997 by The Rosen Publishing Group, Inc.
29 East 21st Street, New York, NY 10010

First Edition

Book Design: Kim Sonsky

Photo Illustrations: Cover and all photo illustrations by Seth Dinnerman.

McGinty, Alice. B.
    Staying Healthy: Good Hygiene / Alice B. McGinty.
    p.   cm. — (The library of healthy living)
    Includes index.
    Summary: Discusses what germs are and how they spread, as well as the importance of being clean and well-groomed.
    ISBN 0-8239-5141-3
    1. Hygiene—Juvenile literature. 2. Health—Juvenile literature. [1. Cleanliness. 2. Grooming. 3. Health.]
I. Title. II. Series.
RA777.M36 1997
613'.4—dc21
                                  96-53252
                                     CIP
                                     AC

Manufactured in the United States of America

Contents

Your Body–Neat and Clean

You have a body to be proud of. It's important to take good care of your body because it has to last for your whole life. Part of taking care of your body means practicing good **hygiene** (HY-jeen)— keeping your body neat and clean.

Good hygiene means washing your body, brushing your teeth, brushing your hair, and trimming your nails. When you do these things, you are learning to take good care of yourself.

Sometimes, though, your body may seem clean to you, but you are still told to wash. Why should you wash when you don't see any dirt?

By practicing good hygiene, you help to keep yourself healthy. You also show the people around you that you care about yourself. ▶

Germs

Even if you don't see dirt on your body, **germs** (JERMZ) may still be there.

Germs are so tiny that you can't see them.

Germs live all around you: on the ground, in the air, on things you touch, and even inside your body.

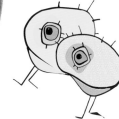

Germs can enter your body with the air you breathe, and through your mouth, eyes, and nose. Your body usually fights the germs inside you. But when too many germs live inside your body, you can get sick. You may get a cold, the flu, chicken pox, or an **infection** (in-FEK-shun).

Real germs are too tiny to see.

A Germ's Best Helper

Your hands are a germ's best helper!

Think of all the things you touch. Your hands touch many things that have germs. Luckily, hands are protected from germs. Your skin acts as a shield to keep germs out.

But hands carry germs around with them. They put germs in your body when you lick your fingers, touch and eat food, rub your eyes, and scratch your nose.

It is important to wash your hands, especially before touching food and after using the bathroom!

Your Skin

Like all living things, your body is made of tiny **cells** (SELZ). Your body is always making new cells that grow and replace the old ones.

Your skin is made of billions of cells. There are two layers in your skin. The top layer is called the **epidermis** (ep-uh-DER-mis). It is made of dead skin cells. The layer of skin below the epidermis is called the **dermis** (DER-mis). This layer is made of new cells.

The new cells in the dermis push the old cells up, where they become a part of the epidermis. There, the old cells flatten and die. These old cells flake away as other, newer cells reach the top.

Whenever anything rubs your skin, old skin cells come off. This helps keep your skin soft and smooth.

The old, dry cells fall off whenever you rub or scratch your skin.

Under Your Skin

Many things are happening under your skin.

☺ New cells are being made.

☺ Hairs are growing from tiny tubes called **hair follicles** (HAYR FOL-ih-kulz).

12

Diagram labels: hair, epidermis, nerve, dermis, sweat gland, fat cells, blood vessels

Can you see hairs growing on your skin?
☺ **Oil glands** (OYL GLANDZ) are making oil to keep your skin soft.
☺ Sweat is being made by **sweat glands** (SWET GLANDZ) to cool your body. Your sweat comes out through tiny holes in your skin called pores.

☺ **Blood vessels** (BLUD VES-ulz) are bringing food and water to your skin cells.

☺ **Nerve fibers** (NERV FY-berz) are helping you to feel the things you touch. They also help you feel heat and cold.

◀ *In one square inch of skin, there are 94 oil glands, 19 feet of blood vessels, 625 sweat glands, and 19,000,000 cells.*

13

Your Hair

Hair is made from dead cells too. New cells form in the hair follicles. They push older cells up, making your hair grow about half an inch each month.

Brushing your hair is important. It does more than just untangle your hair. Brushing also spreads oil from your scalp to the ends of hairs to keep them healthy.

Each day, 50 to 100 hairs fall out of your head and new hairs replace them.

hair

hair muscle

hair follicle

Everyone's hair is different—dry, oily, straight, curly, dark, light, short, or long. What do you like about your hair? ▶

Fingernails and Toenails

Fingernails and toenails are made from dead, hardened cells. They grow as new cells form. Your growing nails need to be trimmed. If your toenails grow too long, your shoes won't fit. And fingernails that are too long can scratch someone by mistake.

Trim fingernails into a smooth, oval shape.

Trim
your toenails
straight across the top.

Biting your nails can tear skin and make nails ragged and sharp. It is much better to trim them.

Nails and **cuticles** (KEW-tih-kulz), or the skin around your nails, need to be cleaned gently. Dirt and germs can collect underneath them.

Your Teeth

When germs in your mouth combine with sugar from food, they make **acid** (A-sid). Acid eats away at your teeth. If it stays on your teeth too long, it can make holes or **cavities** (KAV-ih-teez). This is called tooth **decay** (dih-KAY).

You can protect your teeth from tooth decay. How? By brushing your teeth and gums every morning, after meals, and before bed. This way you can scrub away germs, sugar, and acid.

It is a good idea to use **dental floss** (DEN-tul FLOSS) every day. Flossing with dental floss cleans between your teeth and on your gums.

Brush the front, sides, backs, and tops of your teeth. ▶

It's important
to visit your
dentist for
regular
checkups
too.

What Would Happen?

Cleaning your body washes away many things you cannot see: germs, sweat, oil, old skin cells, dirt, and acid. These things need to be washed away. What if you didn't wash them away?

It's very easy to practice good hygiene, and it ▶
helps you to feel, smell, and look great.

Sweat and old cells would collect dirt and your body would smell bad. Your skin could get rashes or sores. Oil would collect on your hair and skin. Your hair would get oily and limp. Germs could make you sick. Acid on your teeth would make cavities and give you bad breath.

By practicing good hygiene, you can keep yourself clean, neat, and healthy!

◀ *If you did not take care of your body by washing regularly, you would look, smell, and feel dirty!*

Being Neat and Clean

How can you keep yourself neat and clean?

☺ Wash your body with soap. Soap attaches to dirt and oils and washes them away.

☺ Shampoo your hair and brush it. This will make it soft and shiny. Getting haircuts often will keep you looking neat.

☺ Clean and trim your nails, and brush and floss your teeth.

Take care of your body. If you do, you will look good and feel proud of the way you look!

Glossary

acid (A-sid) A substance that is made from germs and sugar, and decays teeth.

blood vessel (BLUD VES-ul) A tunnel that carries blood through your body.

cavity (KAV-ih-tee) A soft spot or hole in a tooth.

cell (SEL) A tiny living piece that all living things are made of.

cuticle (KEW-tih-kul) The skin around your nails.

decay (dih-KAY) When acid eats away at a tooth and damages it.

dental floss (DEN-tul FLOSS) A waxy thread used to clean between teeth.

dermis (DER-mis) The layer of skin that is made up of new cells.

epidermis (ep-uh-DER-mis) The top layer of skin which is made up of old cells.

germ (JERM) A tiny living thing that can cause sickness and infection.

hair follicle (HAYR FOL-ih-kul) A tiny tube in which hair begins to grow.

hygiene (HY-jeen) Keeping your body neat and clean.

infection (in-FEK-shun) When a part of your body is taken over by germs.

nerve fiber (NERV FY-ber) A tiny string of cells that senses touch, heat, and cold.

oil gland (OYL GLAND) A tiny sack that makes and releases oil.

sweat gland (SWET GLAND) A tiny sack that makes and releases sweat.

Index